HAYES PRESS

The Call of Christ

Contents

Foreword

There are times when every Christian believer feels a sense of dissatisfaction with his or her life of discipleship (as the Apostle Paul did in Romans 7). So, those of us who love the Lord and value our Bibles will from time to time be motivated to explore afresh the character of radical discipleship as opposed to pew-filling, sermon– tasting comfortable 'churchianity' which for many can end up as a sort of passive, if not pious, 'spectator sport.'

To start with, the Bible never encourages us to think of ourselves simply as those who have 'made a decision for Christ'. Why not? It is because the actual reality is so much more wonderful than that - as we are reminded early on in this book. Our life of discipleship has been part of God's long-term plan, ripening from all eternity. It's designed to result in us being 'siblings for God's Son' with the privilege and responsibility of touching others' lives for eternity. This is life's great purpose; it's what gives it true meaning.

The dying Buddha asked his disciples not to remember him – only his teaching counted. With Jesus Christ, it is not only His teaching that counts, but also a personal allegiance to Christ the teacher. Christianity is outstandingly about being in a living relationship with its divine founder. We are to be committed to

Jesus as His witnesses, and directed by Him as worshippers of His Father. This is so much more than a mere philosophy or a help through life.

In the New Testament lives of the first disciples, two temptations crippled the spirit of service. They were exemplified in the status-seeking of James and John (Mat. 20:21); and the self-pity of Peter (Luke 18:28). As we grow older it becomes easier to look for privilege, position and respect, but in our review of biblical discipleship within the confines of this book, we are reminded that true service occurs when we are ambitious for God's kingdom alone. That happens when we are God-centred, and sustained by His all-sufficient grace in the midst of human frailty. In other words, when we are servants like the Lord who has called us to Himself in order for us to be like Him.

There is a view of Christianity abroad today which denies anything negative as being in God's plan for our lives. Success and prosperity are lauded as supreme virtues. The problem with this is that it is so foreign to biblical discipleship. The obedient first disciples of Christ, like their God-honouring Master, suffered physical persecution, mental and emotional pain, as well as spiritual grief.

Their suffering for Christ's sake extended in many cases even to their death. The Lord may not ask the same of us in physical terms, but uncompromising obedience will never be anything other than uncomfortable.

Whether it's giving of our self or giving of our stuff, it remains true that it's more blessed to give than to receive. Christian discipleship is about owning very practically in our lives the lordship of Christ. All that we have is now no longer our own. We recognize that what we have is in trust from the Lord to use in His service. Perhaps personal discipleship is never more challenging than when we honestly try to work out the difference between relying on things and depending on the Lord. So it is useful to have our attention drawn by one contributing author to people in both Old and New Testaments who have blazed a trail for us in this.

In a world today that would so often tend to value personal happiness way above personal holiness, it comes as something of a reality check, if not a culture shock, to notice again that the call of God sets us apart in His sight as holy, and obliges us most definitely to live holy lives in this defiling world. That means being very alert to the fact that we can become desensitized to God's standards while acclimatizing to the world's by uncritically absorbing ourselves in the output of television and internet and the less attractive side of the expanding world of social networking. Now there's yet another challenge!

The Rabbis of Jesus' day would have accepted disciples only from the ranks of the ceremonially clean, from the righteous according to the law, and from those of sufficient intelligence to study the Torah with a view to becoming Rabbis themselves. By contrast, Jesus called a curious cross-section of contemporary society: down-to-earth fishermen; zealots; despised turn-coats; a mix of Greek and Semitic names; and with perhaps a Judean along with Galileans – a microcosm of Judaism at that time.

This cosmopolitan range was to be typical rather than accidental, for the call to Christ in discipleship is a call to a shared discipleship. By this we mean that the Lord calls us to share our lives with Him and with one another in love. Discipleship is a challenge not to be faced alone – and some of the others we are to share our lives with come from very different backgrounds to our own!

Speaking of challenges, modern evangelism has been criticized for calling many to belief, but few to obedience; whereas biblical evangelism – 'discipleship evangelism' - centres on the Kingdom of God, stresses the rule of God, and calls people to radical obedience. Unlike other radical cells in contemporary society, perhaps we need to ask ourselves if we are setting the bar too low? The question demands an answer, and this book addresses it.

For sure, Christians are meant to be in the world, but the world is not meant to be in Christians! Sadly, worldliness in some form often encroaches on our lives, and sometimes it takes the form of us becoming infected with the attitude that demands· 'What's in it for me?' What has happened? We have become 'me-centred' rather than 'Christ-centred'. Now it's thrillingly true that we have been given a hope and an inheritance in Christ. However, it is only right that we spend time thinking about what's in it for God in terms of our lives as Christ's disciples.

It is always good to finish on a high, and we certainly do that in this course. The high point of our discipleship is our worship experience among God's people. As we journey through the modules which together present us with a biblical kaleidoscope of discipleship, what comes into focus is the fact that the call to Christ is the call to God's community, and that in turn is the call to worship (and what a worship experience it truly is, as described in the final module). Such a mind-blowing privilege explains – and renders so worthwhile - the high demands of true biblical discipleship which all the contributions making up this book present us with.

Read, think, act.

1

Called by Christ – Karl Smith

I was never much good at games. Every week in the winter months I would stand in line at school as captains picked their football teams, not really listening for my name since I knew it would be among the last to be called. I wasn't particularly bothered. I'd accepted fairly early on that football wasn't my thing. Nevertheless, it was always nice if my name was, say, the nineteenth to be called and I was not left until the very last!

If you are a believer in the Lord Jesus Christ, He has chosen you and called you by name. When you put your trust in Him, you stepped forward and accepted your place on His team. You are not a last resort. For reasons you'll probably never understand, you were the one He wanted, chosen in Him before the foundation of the world, that we should be holy and blameless before him (Ephesians 1:4). Of course you had a decision of your own to make, to accept His offer of grace, but He had already chosen you, as shown in John 15:16: "You did not choose me, but I chose you and appointed you that you should go and bear fruit and that your fruit should abide ..."

The purpose of the call and its place in the scheme of things is given in Romans 8:28-29: "And we know that for those who love God all things work together for good, for those who are called according to his purpose. For those whom he **foreknew** he also **predestined** to be conformed to the image of his Son, in order that he might he the firstborn among many brothers. And those whom he predestined he also **called**, and those whom he called he also **justified**, and those whom he justified he also **glorified**." The purpose is underlined and the five steps by which it is achieved are in bold type.

God is assembling a team of siblings for His Son, people who are allowed to become like Him. There is no higher destiny. Whom does He call to this wonderful transformation? Those whom He has predestined. And who are they? They are those whom He foreknew from His vantage point outside time. What happens after He has called them? He justifies them, declaring that they are righteous because His Son's righteousness qualified Him alone to bear the punishment on the cross for their unrighteousness. Then they are glorified, changed to reflect the moral glories of the Lord Jesus' character and given the hope of entering fully into all His glory in heaven. If you have a Christlike character, you will produce fruit, including the beautiful fruit of the Spirit that marked the Lord's own character, as listed in Galatians 5. The work you do for Him will have lasting results that will never be erased from the lives you touch with the love of Christ. The modules in this course will point you to some of the purposes for which He has called you.

Think of the twelve apostles. They were among the many people fascinated by Jesus of Nazareth, but one day "he went up on the mountain and called to him those whom he desired, and they came to him ... so that they might be with him" (Mark 3:13,14). How privileged they must have felt. Of course He had called them there to send them on a special and unique mission as apostles. Nevertheless, as we have seen from Ephesians, He calls you and me to be with Him, to spend time with Him, to be His disciples, to bear lasting fruit for Him in our lives. Notice, too, that there is a direction to this call: "I chose you out of the world" (John 15:19).

If you are on the M6 motorway in England, driving towards Carlisle, you are necessarily driving away from Birmingham. The Lord Jesus has chosen you out of the world. If you have responded to that call, keep your back to the temptations of the world and your face towards the One who has called you. Christian reader, you need never feel that your life has no value. Christ Himself has chosen you and called you for a purpose. You have something to get on with.

Bible quotations from the ESV.

For further study:

1. Try to describe in your own words the sense of privilege and value that comes from considering the fact that we have been specifically called and chosen by Christ.
2. How does this help us to keep our back towards temptation?
3. Counsellors make a lot of the basic human need for 'significance'. How does the thrust of this first section address that?
4. The over-arching purpose behind God's call is presented

here from Romans 8 as our being conformed to the image of Christ so that He might be pre-eminent among many brothers. Try to describe the impact of such an overwhelming realisation: namely, that God has assembled us into a team of siblings for His Son.

5. To which of the five steps of Romans 8:28-30 is the development of a Christlike character related? Is the associated fruitfulness a matter of 'being' or 'doing' - or both?

6. How much is our enjoyment of the value of such a life bound up with the attention we place on 'being with Him' (spending time daily with Him as His disciples)?

2

Called to Jesus – Greg Neely

Whom do you resemble – your mother, your father, a famous person ... the dog? Are your features, your expressions, your mannerisms, your walk, your sense of humour so much like them (okay, not the dog!) that others immediately notice the similarities? That's what the call to Jesus involves: looking and sounding and acting like the One who has called us to Himself.

The kind of speech that betrayed Peter just before he betrayed Jesus should clearly declare the person with whom we have been as well. 'Jehovah is salvation' –that is the meaning of the name 'Jesus'; a transliteration of the Hebrew name 'Joshua.'[1] In incarnation, that is the name God gave His Son because that describes exactly why God was manifested in the flesh. No Jesus, no salvation – not only for Israel, but also for us! Without salvation through faith in Jesus, life is a few short years of vanity followed by an eternity of calamity. Not only so, but the life we now live in the flesh, good though it might be for many,

---

[1] (1) W.E. Vine, An Expository Dictionary of New Testament Words

cannot be experienced at its best. But Jesus came to show what the unsearchable God is like in terms humans can search out (John 1:18) so that we believe on Him and look and act like Him (Romans 8:29; Colossians 3:10).

He has done His part perfectly and completely. We have been saved to the uttermost; that cannot get any better! Song of Solomon now what? Jesus said to His disciples: "... but you will receive power when the Holy Spirit has come upon you; and you shall be My witnesses ... even to the remotest part of the earth" (Acts 1:8). Like it or not, we are His witnesses. Being a witness does not depend on whether or not we open our mouths and declare what we have witnessed. We are witnesses de facto because we are saved. But what are we doing about our commitment to accurately and enthusiastically declare who and what we have witnessed? If we have truly seen Jesus, Jehovah our Saviour, hanging on a cross, bearing our sins in His own body; if we have truly accepted Him as Lord and Saviour; if we have truly appreciated His awesome substitutionary sacrifice for us, then in loving appreciation we will speak about what we know. And His Spirit, the Spirit of Christ, ignites the dynamic power within us to do what God wants us to do for Him.

Have you pledged your allegiance to Jesus? Implicitly, we have pledged allegiance to our country and its flag and political leader. By comparison, wonderful though those might be, they are nothing compared with the One who has purchased our pardon. At salvation, pledging allegiance to Him is what you were doing! As you were immersed in water when you were baptized, that is what you were doing! If you have missed one of those experiences, you know where to start. But have you given yourself fully to Him today? Being called to Jesus is not a religious, Sunday activity. He is not simply your focus on Sunday and a haze from Monday to Saturday. He is your life, your breath, your strength, your all. He demands no less; you can give Him no more. Too often we hear well-meaning teachers tell us that Jesus must be first in our lives.

But that's not right! He must be our lives! He is not a priority. He is the fulcrum in our lives upon which all our priorities must hinge. No wonder Paul stated: "For to me, to live is Christ and to die is gain (Philippians 1:21) and ... that I may know Him and the power of His resurrection and the fellowship of His sufferings, being conformed to His death. (Philippians 3:10) No wonder Peter could exhort ... but grow in the grace and knowledge of our Lord and Saviour Jesus Christ" (2 Peter 3:18). This is what is involved in our call to Jesus. He's anticipating not just a delightful meeting in the air when He comes. He is excitedly awaiting our meeting with Him today in His word, in conversation, in listening and communion, in meditation, in obedience, in choosing Him to follow today. Have you been in touch with Him?

The Holy Spirit infuses us with power at salvation. He did the same for the early disciples in Jerusalem. The fear and consternation in evidence in the locked upper room on the Sunday of His resurrection showed the weakness of men whose lives had been shattered by the death of the One they thought was their Saviour. The tears of Mary in the garden reveal the brokenness of her heart, and her words to the angels her confusion and sorrow: "... they have taken away my Lord, and I do not know where they have laid Him" (John 20:13). Her grief caused her not to recognize Him when He stood before her. The two on the way to Emmaus had had such high hopes that this Jesus was the One who would redeem Israel. But those hopes had been dashed at His death - or so they thought until they recognized Him.

What a difference seeing Jesus in resurrection made to them! What a difference it can make to us as well! Yes, He died and was buried. Praise God for that. But He is alive! The One who calls us to Himself to imitate His character is not simply a historical figure to be known by literary scholarship. He is a living Saviour who communicates with us through the living Word so that, in devotion to Him, we may actually know Him, not just know about Him. The locked doors on Sunday in Jerusalem were wide open on Monday!

The plaintive cry of Mary to the angels became the ecstatic shout, "Rabboni!" to the Saviour. The dashed hopes of the two travellers became delightful hallelujahs as their eyes were opened to recognize Him. And what did they do with their new-found exuberance? They told other people about the One whose resurrection had completely thrilled them! And they did not even have the Holy Spirit indwelling them yet for almost another two months! We have Him resident within us. If we find it difficult to speak about the One to whom we have pledged our allegiance, perhaps we need to witness again His misery, His mercy and His majesty. When we marvel at His magnificence, we'll speak of Him in superlatives to others.

"Beloved, now we are children of God, and it has not appeared as yet what we will be" (1 John 3:2). Do we look, speak and act like God's children? It's going to get better in immeasurable and incomprehensible ways! We know that when He appears, we will be like Him, because we will see Him just as He is. How big a change is going to take place in you and me? Isaiah there a hint now in our character and conduct of the wonder of that transformation to come? There should be! 'And everyone who has this hope fixed on Him purifies himself, just as He is pure' (1 John 3:3). Whose we are determines what we should be. For we have been called to a relationship, not a religion. We have been called to a person, 'the only begotten God who is in the bosom of the Father' (John 1:18). And that person is Jesus who came to show us God: "He has explained Him." Because He has explained Him, shown Him to us so vividly in His life, we can explain Him to others in how we live and in what we say.

'If your tongue is not like angels',
If you cannot preach like Paul,
You can tell the Saviour's goodness,
You can say He died for all.
If you cannot rouse the wicked
With the judgment's dread alarms,
You can lead the little children
To the Saviour's waiting arms '
(Dr D. March)

But we'll only do it in the power of the Holy Spirit when our lives and words are consistent with and passionate about the One to whom we have pledged our allegiance. Whom do you resemble today? You've been called to Jesus. Can others tell?

Bible quotations from the NASB.

For further study:

1. In what ways can we practically pledge our allegiance to Jesus?
2. With a friend, compare notes about any hints you see in each other's character and conduct of the coming transformation (1 John 3:2)?
3. What difference ought it to make that we have been called to a relationship, not a religion?
4. Is being a witness a gift for some or a responsibility for all?
5. What incentives or motivations for effective witnessing for Christ has this section clarified for you?

3

Called to Community – Craig Jones

He wasn't there - again! Despite otherwise full pews, the empty space just seemed to glare at him. Perhaps it was because the man who usually sat there had done so faithfully every week for as many years as the pastor could remember. How many weeks had it been empty now – two or three? He decided there and then that he must pay the man a visit that afternoon. He lived alone in a small cottage and as the pastor knocked on the door, it was opened almost immediately, as if the occupant were expecting a visit. After exchanging pleasantries they both sat down beside the open fire in the living room, which brought a welcome warmth to the situation. Nothing was said. They both just sat there, gazing into the vivid amber glow of the fire. It didn't even feel as awkward as the pastor had feared.

After a few more minutes, he reached forward and took the tongs from the fireplace set and with them carefully removed a glowing, red hot ember and placed it on the hearth stone. Both men fixed their gaze on it, watching as its glow faded so that all that was left was a charred black coal. The pastor took the tongs and placed the coal back into the fire, where it immediately began to glow again, until it was once more red hot. Another minute or two passed, then the pastor got up and made his way to the door. The other man also got up and helped the pastor on with his coat. Not a word had been said since they sat down in front of the fire. As he was going out the door the pastor turned around to say goodbye, but, with tears in his eyes, the man simply looked at him and said, "Thank you so much for visiting and thank you for your fiery sermon. I'll see you back at church again next Sunday."[2]

Paul Simon, of folk pop duo 'Simon and Garfunkel' fame, wrote a song in 1965 called 'I Am a Rock' and, for many fans of the duo, it is amongst their finest productions.

> I am a rock,
> I am an island.
> I've built walls,
> A fortress deep and mighty,
> That none may penetrate.

Clearly written from some painful personal experience, the lyrics nevertheless have resonated with many people through the years, giving expression, some would say, to the increasingly insular, selfish, 'me-centred' attitude that characterises many societies, leading to a breakdown in community values. Comparison - or rather, contrast - is often made with the work of the Elizabethan poet John Donne, who wrote the following in 1624: No man is an island, entire of itself; every man is a piece

---

[2] Author unknown

of the continent, part of the main. If a clod be washed away by the sea, Europe is the less ...[3]

From a biblical perspective, John Donne is much nearer the mark than Paul Simon, in giving expression to an essential aspect of human nature. The fact of the matter is, we were created by God to be inter-dependent, not independent. It's a foundational principle of human relationships, which was expressed way back in the Garden of Eden when God observed, "It is not good for the man to he alone; I will make him a helper suitable for him" (Genesis 2:18). This sense of the need for companionship, and the value of 'being together', is a theme that is central to God's dealings with mankind. All His revealed purposes through Abraham to Moses were centred on the establishment of a community of believers who would come together in unity of heart and purpose - and in obedience to what God had said about how they should achieve that - in order to serve Him, in close relationship with Him and with each other. That community of believers was known as 'the people of God' and their direct relationship with God was clearly and repeatedly expressed in the Old Testament, when God referred to them as My people.

It's not in the least bit surprising, then, to find that same value and importance of 'community' given renewed emphasis in the New Testament, amongst those who believed in the Lord Jesus Christ. Jesus went to great lengths to get that point across to His disciples in the hours just before His crucifixion, showing us the value He Himself placed upon it. In that upper room, He

---

[3]   For Whom the Bell Tolls, Devotions Upon Emergent Occasions, Meditation XVII, (1624)

spoke about what those men would have to face after He was gone - the challenges, the trials, the heartache (John 13 - John 17). He also revealed to them that they wouldn't be alone in it, that they would have His presence with them, through the indwelling Holy Spirit (John 14:18,26; John 16:7,13-14). And He also gave them a new commandment, which was to be a defining characteristic of this new community of believers, and which expresses the most basic unifying power that would achieve the Lord's vision; "A new commandment I give to you, that you love one another, even as I have loved you ... My this all men will know that you are My disciples" (John 13:34-35).

Those first disciples, and therefore those who subsequently believe through them, were called to be a community of believers, actively living out the things taught to them by the Lord, as they bore witness to His saving grace - and the underpinning of that community was a mutual love, a quality of love which is divine in origin and which found practical expression in their inter-dependence (John 17:20). They certainly took that new commandment to heart, as we observe them coming together for mutual support and encouragement in those days immediately following the Lord's ascension (Acts 1:14; Acts 2:1).

Out of love, they provided for each others' practical needs: "All those who had believed were together and had all things in common ... sharing them with all, as anyone might have need. Day by day continuing with one mind ...taking their meals together with gladness and sincerity of heart, praising God ... And the Lord was adding to their number ..." (Acts 2:44-47; see also Acts 4:32-35).

When the expected persecution came, they supported each other in prayer (Acts 12:5). When problems came that threatened their treasured unity, they looked to one another for the answers (Acts 6:1-6; Acts 15:1-31). The love of the Lord both in terms of its origin and their sharing of it - was key to it all. Paul, Peter, James and John all highlighted its vital importance in their writings (see 1 Corinthians 13:1-13; 1 Peter 1:22,4:8; James 2:8; 1 John 4:7-21).

You and I need each other. In our love for the Lord, in our faith, in our striving to live for Him, we need each other's support and encouragement - and that of our other brothers and sisters in the Lord. When we try to 'go it alone' or when we don't give priority to being with fellow-believers, the glow of our love, enthusiasm and commitment to the Lord will rapidly fade and grow cold. How often have you been encouraged by a fellow-disciple's joy in the Lord? How often have you received the sound, wise advice of an older Christian? How many times have you been helped and comforted through some difficult situation by the shared experience of another Christian?

These examples, and many more besides, show how our inter-dependence is essential to our spiritual growth and development. A loving, supportive community is what the Lord has called us to - a unity of heart and purpose, which, following Christ's own example, does not merely look out for our own personal interests, but those of others as well (Philippians 2:4).

And there is no room for a 'lowest common denominator' approach to achieving this all-important oneness, which is the Lord's expressed desire for all His disciples: "... that they may all be one ..." (John 17:20-23). It cannot be achieved on the basis of our own set of ground-rules or guidelines. It can only successfully be achieved by a sincere commitment to obediently following the pattern that the Lord has laid out in His Word (Romans 6:17; 2 Timothy 1:13). When the Lord calls us to Himself, He calls us as individuals and opens our heart to receive His precious gift of forgiveness through Christ. But that's not the end of it-not at all! He then shows us how we should come together with other believers who have the same love and the same desire to follow obediently (Acts 2:41,42).

This unity is so important to the Lord, and therefore it must also be important for us to make sure we are giving effect to it by being in a community with those who are already obediently putting it into practice, according to God's Word.

Bible quotations from the NASB.

For further study:

1. Where, and in what ways, does God establish the value of 'community' in the Old Testament?
2. How does the chapter - and Scripture - illustrate the dangers of 'going it alone'?
3. Share (or reflect on) a time when you've been helped by another disciple. What Bible text did this help illuminate?
4. In what ways is it made clear by the chapter that there is a prescribed Biblical pattern for the community life to which we are called?

4

Called to Serve – David Webster

Have you ever wondered what Peter's wife said when he told her he was giving up his job to follow Jesus of Nazareth? Or what Zebedee thought when James and John announced that they were leaving the family business? Maybe they went with their family's blessing, or perhaps they went despite their opposition. We don't know, of course, but Peter and John were both certain that they had received a real 'call' (something like a summons or invitation) from the Lord Jesus to serve and they were aware of something of the cost of that, as well as of the excitement and opportunity.

There would inevitably be excitement and no doubt a real 'buzz' from being with the Lord Jesus! The disciples would savour those good days when the crowds were coming in their droves and they witnessed "... a great number of people from all over Judea, from Jerusalem, and from the coast of Tyre and Sidon, who had come to hear him and to be healed of their diseases. Those troubled by evil spirits were cured, and the people all tried to touch him, because power was coming from him and healing them all" (Luke 6:17-19).

It was Peter and John, together with James, who were privileged to see things that others only heard about: they witnessed the Lord Jesus raising up the daughter of Jairus the synagogue ruler even while the mourners were wailing for her! They were present when the Lord Jesus healed Peter's mother-in-law, who was in bed with a fever; and Peter wrote about being '…eye-witnesses of his majesty. For he received honour and glory from God the Father when the voice came to him from the Majestic Glory, saying, "This is my Son, whom I love; with him I am well pleased." We ourselves heard this voice that came from heaven when we were with him on the sacred mountain' (2 Peter 1:16-18).

But it wasn't all excitement and enjoying the approval of the crowds when the disciples of the Lord Jesus were called to serve. The Lord Jesus never promised the disciples that they would get an easy life, or that they would become celebrities! In the three years they spent with the Master they discovered how hard it was to be associated with the man from Nazareth (see John 1:46), the teacher who would not conform to the accepted ways (see Matthew 9:11) or the stone you builders rejected, as Peter, later, charged the Jewish leaders (Acts 4:11). But, of course, the Lord Jesus reminded them of this: "Remember the words I spoke to you: 'No servant is greater than his master.' If they persecuted me, they will persecute you also. If they obeyed my teaching, they will obey yours also" (John 15:20).

Getting too excited

The Lord Jesus had sent His disciples out with authority to "Heal the sick who are there and tell them, 'The kingdom of God is near you'" (Luke 10:9). It seems they had a good time and the mission was a success. They returned to the Lord in buoyant mood, "Lord, even the demons submit to us in your name" (Luke 10:17). But the Lord sensed that their excitement was in danger of taking over so that what they could see and feel might gain more importance than fundamental spiritual truths. "Rejoice," said the Master, "that your names are written in heaven" (Luke 10:20). We must never become so involved in service that we forget to say 'Thanks' to our Lord for our salvation. Service begins with recognising what the Lord has done for us in reaching out to save us.

Getting too self-absorbed

I wonder if Peter was having a bad day! The Lord Jesus was talking about how hard it is for the rich to enter the kingdom of God and the conversation progressed to whether anyone could be saved. "Is it an impossibility?" some wondered. Maybe Peter thought the Lord's message was too much, so he blurted out, "We have left all we had to follow you!" (Luke 18:28) Was he comparing the way the disciples had responded to the lack of response of the wealthy man? Or was he feeling sorry for himself? The Lord expects would–be disciples to count the cost, but those already on the disciple path should not be looking back to opportunities lost or consoling themselves with the thought that they can impress the Lord with the things they have given up. Service continues with a willingness to give up everything and not to look back with disappointment at what we have given up.

Getting too self-centred

Jockeying for position, getting your request in first, staking a claim to the best seat or just presenting a logical case for your own advancement! We see it all the time in politics, the business world, and in celebrities as they seek publicity. Disciples of the Lord Jesus are different, of course – or are we? James and John's agent in this was their mother! Her request was as stark as it was inappropriate! "Grant that one of these two sons of mine may sit at your right and the other al your left in your kingdom" (Matthew 20:21).

The Lord saw the naked ambition of the two brothers and challenged them with a question they barely understood, "Can you drink the cup I am going to drink?" (Matthew 20:22). Having made their claim there was no backing down. "We can." Was it bravado? Was it an attempt to impress? They had no idea what the cup the Lord Jesus was about to drink was; thankfully they could never drink that nor can any of us. The Lord Jesus had a path of service assigned to Him and it was His very food to stick to it (John 4:34). Service is fulfilled by accepting the place to which the Lord has assigned us and not trying to outmanoeuvre others.

Getting too concerned about others

"What about him?" We are often not satisfied until we've found out what everyone else has been assigned to do. That's natural, but it must not get in the way of our service for the Master. Peter, having let the Lord down, was graciously reinstated. The Lord had probed him about his love, told him some details about where his service would take him, indicated service through to old age and even indicated the manner of his death. Perhaps Peter was overwhelmed by it all and just wanted to know what the Lord intended for his friend John.

'Peter turned and saw that the disciple whom Jesus loved was following them. (This was the one who had leaned back against Jesus at the supper and had said, "Lord, who is going to betray you?") When Peter saw him, he asked, "Lord, what about him?"' (John 21:20-21). The Lord's reply was a call to focus on what we are called to do. As Master, the Lord Jesus has the right to assign any of us to any role. Jesus answered, "If I want him to remain alive until I return, what is that to you? You must follow me" (John 21:22). Real service for the Master involves us taking instructions from the Lord Jesus without concerning ourselves with what others are called to do.

Ambition

Although the Lord Jesus showed His disappointment at the self-seeking of James and John, He did not disapprove of ambition altogether. It depends what we are ambitious for. The Lord contrasted the worldly desire for power and to get higher than those around by saying: "You know that the rulers of the

Gentiles lord it over them, and their high officials exercise authority over them. Not so with you. Instead, whoever wants to become great among you must be your servant, and whoever wants to be first must be your slave just as the Son of Man did not come to be served, but to serve, and to give his life as a ransom for many" (Matthew 20:25–28). Followers of the Master must have these attitudes, ambitions and aspirations, as they put God's kingdom first (Matthew 6:33) and with deeply thankful hearts offer themselves in service to the King.

Bible quotations from the NIV.

For further study:

1. Do we tend to search for, or feed off, the wrong kind of excitement in our discipleship experience?
2. Do we tend to embrace losses or look back regretfully on what has been passed up for the sake of Christ?
3. In what ways does it seem to matter to us what others are called to do?
4. What things by nature are we ambitious for? What things should we ambitious for?

5

Called To Simple Dependence On God – Geoff Hydon

A good example

She is famous among almost every group of Christians. She was disadvantaged, yet she did more than many of her generation. No, we are not talking about Mother Teresa. The woman in question is the widow the Lord Jesus watched, as she gave money to Him (Luke 21:1-4). Well, you might think she gave it to the temple, or its leaders, or some good cause, but He knew she was giving it to God. If we appreciate that fully, it might affect the generosity of our giving. This humble woman was just doing what all Israelites were called to do: to love God with everything and their neighbour as themselves (Deuteronomy 6:5).

It is really no different for followers of Christ (Luke 10:25-27). We too are chosen and called (Romans 8:29,30), and called to become like Him. The Lord Jesus made it clear that He chose disciples to be completely dependent on Him, as He Himself surrendered all to God (John 4:34; John 6:38; John 9:4); that is one of the primary lessons of the well-known passage in John 15 about branches remaining in the Vine (John 15:4,16).

Remember also that the Lord cursed the fig tree that kept the goodness it received for its leaves instead of bearing fruit (Mark 11:13,14). Likewise our problem surely is that we are tempted so much to keep what we have so that we can be self-reliant. But that just brings a false sense of security. We are much better to hold very lightly to material things (1 Corinthians 7:30-31), and value very highly the privilege of giving anything to God, relying on Him to refill our lives with what we need (Hebrews 13:5). After all, He doesn't need our gifts; it is us that need to give (Psalm 50:10-12; Acts 17:24-28; Acts 20:35).

How we approach giving can be like a barometer, measuring our commitment to dependence on God. God measures our giving by what we have left, as evidenced in the case of the poor widow. And in this context two of the things that may restrain our giving are wrong attitudes: firstly, about really who owns all that we have, and secondly, who can best decide how to use it. The widow evidently had a viewpoint that overcame these problems; she surrendered herself to God, the true owner and decision-maker.

Practical wisdom

Are you one of those Bible readers who values a daily aphorism (a short saying, full of practical value)? The book of Proverbs is full of them, and many godly people have included reading a proverb alongside their main reading for the day. Near the end of the book the following saying arises (Proverbs 30:8-9):

> Give me neither poverty nor riches.
> Feed me with the food allotted to me;
> Lest I be full and deny You,
> And say, "Who is the LORD?"
> Or lest I be poor and steal,
> And profane the name of my God.

There is a lot of practical wisdom in these words, and we would do well to approach each day with this desire. It is interesting to note that dependence on God is not restricted to those who are poor. The wealthy are very exposed to an attitude of self-determination. However, Paul knew that both rich and poor alike can find contentment. He says: "I have learned to be content in whatever circumstances I am. I know how to get along with humble means, and I also know how to live in prosperity; in any and every circumstance I have learned the secret of being filled and going hungry, both of having abundance and suffering need. I can do all things through Him who strengthens me" (Philippians 4:11–13 NASB).

So dependence brings contentment, not based on our getting more and becoming self-reliant, but by giving more and finding satisfaction in what God supplies.

No exemptions

We are surely all tested in our dependence on God; you will not bump into anybody who has been exempted! But some will be tested more than others. Greater privilege brings greater responsibility, so we may expect that those who have been given more by God will be tested more in this than those who have least. Song of Solomon it is not surprising to find that a good example in the Old Testament is one of Judah's kings.

King Jehoshaphat had his reliance on God severely tested, but he proved true the New Testament aphorism that 'God is faithful, who will not allow you to be tempted beyond what you are able' (1 Corinthians 10:13). Jehoshaphat's trial included being faced with an enemy army that seemed well able to wipe Judah off the map. In response to prayer, God sent a prophet to tell the king that, contrary to human expectations, victory was secure for Judah. God would fight for them. Now here is the thing that convinces us that Jehoshaphat placed absolute dependence on God. When he sent out his troops, who did he commission to lead them? Singers. Yes, singers; not archers or infantry or charioteers. And as soon as they began to sing praise to God, God kept His word and wiped out the enemy army (2 Chronicles 20:21,22). Jehoshaphat had his failings, and it is true to say that his dependence on God was partly a result of being afraid, but God can use our fears to bring us nearer to Himself.

As the Psalmist said: 'Whenever I am afraid, I will trust in You.' Perhaps some of us would actually benefit from being exposed to loss of some of the things we rely on, so that we would be more ready to depend on God. Certainly it is clear from the Lord's teaching in Matthew 6 that we should not cling to the very temporary pleasures of life, or even the practical 'necessities.' We need to give them a proper place, and seek His kingdom and His righteousness. The Lord also emphasized to those He commissioned to witness for Him that they should travel with the minimum of everyday goods (Luke 10:4). These men went to places they might expect would refuse to welcome them, without taking anything to fall back on. They had to rely on God to provide what they needed, and He did (Luke 10:17)!

A healthy perspective

If we are prone to being too materialistic and self-reliant then, for starters, there are six things that we can instead pursue to combat wrong-headedness about material wealth. These are listed by Paul in his instruction to Timothy on the subject (1 Timothy 6:6-11). He concludes: "But you, O man of God, flee these things (which result from a love of money) and pursue righteousness, godliness, faith, love, patience, gentleness."

You cannot assess these in financial terms. You could try to rate yourself on each of them on a scale of 1-10, and then work on the weakest score. However, we are each susceptible to evaluating ourselves incorrectly, so we had better not try to do this independently. That's not to suggest you or I simply go and ask a friend to do the rating. Rather, I should find myself in the company of the Master, and let Him work upon my spirit to show me how I am doing, and show me what is good for me. Dependence on God cannot be achieved without prayerfully knowing His presence. The Psalmist knew the positive outworking of this when he said: "no good thing will He withhold from those who walk uprightly, for the rest of this psalm is a cry from the heart for nearness to God" (Psalm 84:11).

The churches that came into being after the Lord ascended to heaven were exemplary in their sharing attitude (Acts 2:42-47; 2 Corinthians 8:2). This is the practical outworking of dependence on God. As we depend on Him to supply, we make ourselves available to be part of that chain of His supply to others by sharing what He has given us (2 Corinthians 9:12). We may usefully consider whether the early growth in those churches was partly attributable to the way in which everyone in the church readily shared with everyone else. They gave up title to property, and fund-raised for the needy. James emphasizes the importance of this in our Christian testimony too (James 2:14-17). We give up for a God who measures our giving by what we retain for ourselves. Our sense of need to keep back a great deal to maintain our personal security can become a fatal flaw (as Ananias and Sapphira infamously found out in Acts 5:1-11). We might almost hear the Son over God's house still saying:

> "Bring all the tithes into the storehouse,
> That there may be food in My house,
> And try Me now in this,"
> Says the LORD of hosts,
> "If I will not open for you the windows of heaven
> And pour out for you such blessing
> That there will not be room enough to receive it."
> (Malachi 3:10)

Bible quotations from the NKJV.

For further study:

1. From one viewpoint, the contribution made by Ananias and Sapphira (Acts 5:1) appears quite generous. What therefore was missing in their attitude toward giving to God?
2. What are the linkages between dependence on God and spiritual contentment?

3. Priscilla and Aquila evaluated their lives very unselfishly (Romans 16:3,4). How do we draw the line between demonstrating dependence on God in our service without it becoming bravado?

4. What are the key feature's in Hannah's simple dependence on God to resolve her yearnings for children? (1 Samuel 1,2)

5. David faithfully relied on God in the battle against Goliath (1 Samuel 17). Should we expect amazing support from God if we are lacking in faith that He will indeed marvellously protect us?

6

Called to Suffer – David Viles

Nobody is immune from it. Job, who knew more than most about suffering, observed that 'Man is born to trouble as the sparks fly upward' (Job 5:7). We know it, painfully, when it comes, and we fear it in prospect. Well, we're in good company; even the Lord Jesus, contemplating the cross, pleaded with His Father: "If it is Your will, take this cup away from Me" (Luke 22:42). For the Christian following the Master, suffering is not to be courted: still less self-mortification, with its tendency to inflate pride and inhibit submission to God (Colossians 2:20-23). The Lord Himself taught that it is right for us to pray, "Do not lead us into temptation, but deliver us from the evil one" (Matthew 6:13).

Yet while God will never tempt us (James 1:13), Scripture is uncompromising that God can and does test the individual believer. The book of Job focuses at length on this paradox, while in the New Testament the Lord said, "In the world, you will have tribulation" (John 16:33) - no doubt about it, then: we are called to suffer! Paul adds that every true disciple 'will suffer persecution' (2 Timothy 3:12).

This is a hard imperative in a materialistic and superficial age -it plumbs the depths of the human experience as well as ascending the heights of the divine purpose. It is all too easy to approach suffering in the abstract, with the platitudes of Eliphaz, Bildad and Zophar-dismissed by the anguished Job as miserable comforters (Job 16:2).

Suffering covers, for the believer, a wide spiritual and physical spectrum and an infinite degree (E.g. hatred, exclusion, reviling, calumny - Luke 6:22: chains and plundering - Hebrews 10:34); your suffering is hurtful and is personal to you as mine is to me, but we all share mystically in the suffering which is experienced by every member of the body of Christ (1 Corinthians 12:26). Perhaps you consider the statement no chastening seems to be joyful for the present (Hebrews 12:11 NIV) as an understatement! If so, we can take heart that through the personal, private pain and anguish there is the 'later' of the same verse - 'later on ... it produces a harvest of righteousness and peace for those who have been trained by it.'

We are not alone

Just as a loving parent is caught up in the life of his child, so God is intimately concerned with the well-being of each believer. This goes beyond care and kindness - it extends to a sharing in our experiences, both of suffering and of joy. Take the example of the enslavement of the people of Israel in Egypt. God heard their cry because of their taskmasters, "for I know their sorrows" (Exodus 3:7). He heard because He reveals Himself as sharing in - empathising with - their misery: 'in all their affliction He was afflicted' (Isaiah 63:9). It is immensely comforting -and fundamental to an understanding both of suffering and of how a loving God can presume to test those He loves - to comprehend in wonder that He weeps with those who weep and deigns to suffer alongside us.

The wonder does not end there, of course. Sharing in the human experience from the security of heaven was not enough - creating complete empathy was the purpose of the incarnation of God the Son: 'as the children have partaken of flesh and blood, He Himself likewise shared in the same' (Hebrews 2:14). The fact that the Lord Jesus shares in our humanity extends and reinforces the identification of the Godhead with suffering saints - in that He Himself has suffered ... He is able to aid those who are tempted (Hebrews 2:18). That sharing involved for the Lord of glory the taking of the lowest place - owning through gritty experience the early realities of rejection, homelessness and insecurity and, finally, the humiliation of Calvary.

So, while we rejoice that our ultimate destiny is to be 'like Him' (1 John 3:2), that process of identification must inevitably involve a calling to suffer as we live counter-culturally in obedience to Him. Paul understood clearly the part played by 'fellowship in His sufferings' in attaining to an intimate knowledge of Christ (Romans 8:17; Philippians 3:10), while Peter brings the process of identification full circle just as Christ brought glory to God by His sufferings so do we by our willingness to suffer for Him (John 21:18-19; 1 Peter 2:20). In comparison, they're merely light afflictions (2 Corinthians 4:17)!

Later on...

Ask the average person about suffering and the response will probably be a negative one. While, as we have seen, the disciple will, like anybody else, avoid unnecessary suffering, he or she will discern, as Job did after all his afflictions, 'the end intended by the Lord: that He is very compassionate and merciful' (James 5:11). Throughout Christian history, commentators have marvelled at the ability of the Christian to persist in believing in a good and loving God despite personal pain and suffering. This was no easy task for Job in ancient times (see particularly Job 16), just as it may be a challenge for some called to particularly intense affliction today, even to persecution for His name.

The Bible is unequivocal that there is a divine purpose in suffering - the 'later on' of Hebrews 12:11. Suffering is not in itself the aim - it is only part of God's loving purpose as the master Potter to make of such unpromising clay as you and me 'vessels of mercy ... for glory' (Romans 9:23). These will be no ordinary kitchenware - God has taken, and is taking, infinite pains to transform each one of us into a genuine work of art - 'predestined to be conformed to the image of His Son' (Romans 8:29). To be, as Christ, 'holy and without blame before Him in love' (Ephesians 1:4). There can be no higher, nobler destiny, ornamenting us to share eternity with Him.

Clay, of course, is inanimate and we are not. Sometimes we wander far from the Potter's studio and it takes the loving Potter - who never gives up on us - to jolt us back to our priorities. 'God whispers ... in our pleasures, speaks in our conscience, but shouts in our pains.'[4] Sometimes we need that jolt - only 'later on' do we recognise the peaceable fruit of righteousness as God recommences His work of embellishing our characters (Psalm 119:67).

With some of us, that work may be starting from a very low base. Here we shift the image, from the potter who looks only to the finished result to our loving heavenly Father who loves us for what - and despite what - we are. Unremittingly, inexorably, He changes us, developing our faith and character into that which pleases Him. 'As a man chastens his son, so the Lord your God chastens you' (Deuteronomy 8:5). This statement, again, runs counter to a culture where the concept of fatherhood is rapidly losing meaning, but the Bible is crystal clear - 'without chastening ... then you are illegitimate and not sons' (Hebrews 12:8).

'Later on' the sensitive ('trained') believer will recognise the harvest it produces - a further step towards the righteousness and peace exemplified in the character of Christ. That character - as it fills the believer - is developed in Scripture and by experience. The image changes again, this time to the work of refining the purest gold (Job 23:10). The righteousness and peace of Christ includes patience, experience and hope among other qualities, all springing from the refining effect of tribulation (Romans 5:3-4). Even Paul had to learn that his painful thorn in the flesh was the work of the divine Refiner purging out the dross of human pride (2 Corinthians 12:7-9), proving the reality of a faith tested by fire (1 Peter 1:6-7).

____

[4] C.S. Lewis: The Problem of Pain, Ch.6

As Job found in his suffering, the effects of submission to the will of God cannot be contained - others will be intrigued or inspired. Eternity will reveal how profoundly and fruitfully individual saints have witnessed - usually unknowingly - through their conduct under suffering, and how greatly other saints have been encouraged thereby (2 Corinthians 1:3-5). To 'bless those who persecute you' (Romans 12:14) reflects powerfully the character of Christ 'who suffered ... the just for the unjust' (1 Peter 3:18).

Later, later...

If the Lord had only said 'in the world you will have tribulation', every day of our earthly existence would be bleak. 'But', He continued, 'be of good cheer, I have overcome the world' (John 16:33). The comfort and reassurance of that 'but' are surely incalculable for all believers in their suffering. If we have found Scripture uncompromising in stressing the inevitability of suffering for the Christian, let us rejoice that, time and time again, there is a closely associated emphasis on the glory that shall follow ...later (see, for example, Matthew 10;39; Romans 8:17-18; 1 Peter 4:12-13; 1 Peter 5:10)! Compared with 'the exceeding and eternal weight of glory', our present afflictions are light (2 Corinthians 4:17).

On the other hand, perhaps we might feel our sufferings are genuinely light compared with those of others. But only the Lord knows what the future holds. 'Our Father refreshes us on the journey with some pleasant inns, but will not encourage us to mistake them for home.'[5]

---

[5]   C.S Lewis op cit. Ch.7

Bible quotations from the NKJV.

For further study:

1. How do you persist in believing in a loving God when you experience personal pain?
2. In what way does it help to know that God deigns to suffer alongside us?
3. Discuss the statement that suffering 'plumbs the depths of the human experience as well as ascending the heights of the divine purpose.' How would you sum up in your own words the divine purpose in suffering as revealed in the Bible?
4. Suggest what it means for a Christian believer to experience 'the fellowship of His sufferings' (Phil.3:10).

7

Called As We Are – Ed Neely

God doesn't think and do as we think and do, and clearly He does not think and do as we think He ought: "For My thoughts are not your thoughts, nor are your ways My ways," says the LORD. "For as the heavens are higher than the earth, so are My ways higher than your ways, and My thoughts than your thoughts" (Isaiah 55:8,9). An example of a difference might be seen when God called Abraham to be a father of nations. He gave him a wife who was barren. Eventually, contrary to all nature, he had a son, Isaac, who also received a barren wife. Ultimately, however, Jacob was born. Jacob, Isaac's son, in turn, married a girl that he did not love and another whom he did, but who was also barren. Three barren generations, according to human wisdom, is hardly the way to propagate and populate a multitude of peoples and nations. We simply would not have done things that way! God's ways are not our ways!

Again in the New Testament when God desired to develop a people for Himself, a capable people endowed with wisdom and ability, He began with a very small group of very incapable, unlearned and seemingly undesirable men. Had the religious leaders and the rabbis of the time been garnering disciples, they would have chosen from the ranks of the ceremonially clean, the ones they thought righteous according to the Law, men of sufficient intelligence and interest to study the Torah, perhaps with a view to becoming rabbis themselves, certainly men who were examples to others, who could display sterling disciple qualities; (men whom John the Baptizer through the Spirit's wisdom called 'offspring of vipers' (Matthew 3:7 RV)).

Instead, Jesus, doing His Father's will, called to Himself a curious cross-section of contemporary society: down-to-earth and somewhat self-centred fishermen, more concerned with who was greatest among them than the Great One who walked in their midst; zealots who were in almost constant revolt against the Romans rather than those who were zealous for the things of God; a despised turn-coat tax collector suspected of fleecing rather than feeding God's sheep; and one other who seemed to rob them blind, whose end was destruction. Jesus' twelve disciples excluded His very own family, though after His crucifixion some are named as part of His people. His disciples had a mixture of Greek and Semitic names, perhaps a Judean along with Galileans, indicating a real microcosm of the Judaism of His day.

Nor, as we see, was this to be a unique choosing of disciples, as Paul reminded the Corinthian church: 'For you see your calling, brethren, that not many wise according to the flesh, not many mighty, not many noble, are called. Hut God has chosen the foolish things of the world ... the weak things ... the base things ... the things which are despised ... and the things which are not, to bring to nothing the things which are, that no flesh should glory in his presence' (1 Corinthians 1:26–29).

The wisdom and nobility of this world might have been highly prized by those of Corinth and those like them of Greek and Roman origins who prized their wisdom, but again we are reminded of the vast differences between the ways of God and men. Not only is the word of the cross foolishness to those who are perishing, but God still uses those who might be considered foolish and of no consequence to convey His message, 'fools for Christ's sake' (1 Corinthians 4:10).

It is not the brilliance, strength and nobility of man that can appreciate the plans of God, not human self-confidence, but self-effacing faith that opens for us the narrow way and an understanding of His Word that enables us to realize that we 'have the mind of Christ' (1 Corinthians 2:16). If Christ had chosen His own followers on the basis of human wisdom and good breeding the twelve apostles, the heroes of the New Testament, as well as us might well have been passed by. Instead He chose the very ordinary, turning human understanding and the worldly way of thinking upside down, that He might do extra-ordinary things through His own to His glory and one day receive them - and others through them - into the glorious courts of heaven.

Not only were the unschooled and ignoble called to discipleship and the fellowship of the Son of God, but a long list of those possessed in earlier days of the grossest sins had been likewise called, washed, sanctified, justified in the name of the Lord Jesus and by the Spirit of our God (1 Corinthians 6:9-11), not because

God had any affinity with iniquity, but to demonstrate His grace and mercy and to prove the efficacy of the sacrifice of Christ on their behalf. God has called the dead in transgressions to life in Christ and as those so called we glorify His name.

In the wisdom of God not only has the way of salvation been hidden from the wise and understanding and revealed to babes, but the path of the disciple as well seldom discloses to the unbeliever the glories that shall be and the peace we have now in our hearts. Even the Apostle Paul was considered foolish, was defamed in his ministry, dishonoured, disgraced, reviled, persecuted and considered the off-scouring of all things. He laboured at his own expense, and was sent out as Christ was sent out; a lamb in the midst of wolves, weak for the sake of the weak, a servant of men that his Master might be glorified and the gospel might flourish. At times even reviled among churches that should have known better, he suffered at the hands and tongues of his brethren. His day of acknowledgement and reward awaits God's soon-coming day of recompense.

God, like Paul, does not wish that His message be distorted by association with the things that are so prized by the wisdom of this world. Those things, which James describes as sensual and demonic, are the very antithesis of the wisdom that is from above, which is pure, peaceable, gentle, reasonable, full of mercy and good fruits, unwavering and without hypocrisy (James 3:15, 17). All in the New Testament churches and we ourselves were called as we were;

> 'Just as I am, without one plea,
> But that Thy blood was shed for me,

And that Thou bidd'st me come to Thee,
O Lamb of God, I come!'
(C. Elliott)

It has not yet been revealed what we shall be, but we know that when He is revealed, we shall be like Him (1 John 3:2). In the meantime we should strive daily to be more like Him here and now. That desire, rather than an undue striving to excel in the things of the world, is to be our aim (1 Corinthians 7:17, 24). The Holy Spirit through the Word of God reveals what a balance in these things should be.

We are not, therefore, to continue in the behaviour and character in which we were called. We commence our discipleship as infants in Christ. Then we are taught and begin to grow. We find that the message of the cross which at first attracted us through the Spirit's gracious working contains more than justification. It concerns our sanctification; it concerns a renewal of attitude and action in response to the revelation of God; it calls for righteousness in thought and deed. It teaches us that the way to exaltation is humility and often humiliation, the way of obedience the way to the revealed wisdom of God. Our involvement in this call by Christ is to an active rather than passive participation in what God has called us to, an inclusion in something amazingly and completely different from what is all around us.

We actually talk to God and expect answers! We are invited to bring our praises right into His very sanctuary. We are welcome to discuss our individual concerns, but more than that, when as a people for God we present the fruit of lips making confession to Christ's name (Hebrews 13:15 RV) we join with saints, angels, and heavenly beings, thrilling the heart of God with thoughts of His Son. Thanks be to God that we were called as we were! Thanks be to God that we are not now as we once were! Thanks be to God that there are even better things ahead!

For further study:

1. Why did Christ not choose His followers on the basis of human wisdom?
2. Ought this to promote a passive or active response from us?
3. How does Paul's own testimony of all he gave up (Phil.3:4-8) support his teaching in 1 Corinthians 1:26-29?
4. What cause for praise can we find in the fact that God's calling is like this (see Matt. 11:25)?

8

Called to Obey – James Needham

'No man ever spoke like this Man!' That was the assessment of the officers of the guard sent to arrest the Lord Jesus on the great day of the feast of tabernacles (John 7:46). Their exposure to His teaching may have been brief, but they quickly shared the astonishment of the crowds at Him who 'taught them as one having authority' (Matthew 7:29). His authority derived from the conviction and wisdom with which He spoke, the signs which accompanied His teaching and the unfailing precision with which He carried out everything He taught. Yet, above all these things, the unparalleled authority which characterised the Lord Jesus had a more fundamental origin, for the one who enraptured the crowds and enthralled the guardsmen of His enemies was none other than the eternal Son of God.

The authority of God

The Scriptures consistently assert the authority of God. Its foundation is in who He is; its claim through His combined works of creation and redemption (Deuteronomy 32:4,6,10-12).

Today, the Lord Jesus bears this authority as 'the heir of all things through whom God has effected His great creative and redemptive works' (Hebrews 1:2-3). His investiture with this supremacy occurred in the eternal ages before He was revealed in flesh, for by the time of His ministry 'the Father had given all things into His hands.' (John 13:3). He could declare that 'all things have been delivered to Me by My Father' (Matthew 11:27) and 'all authority has been given to Me in heaven and on earth' (Matthew 28:18). This was an authority He displayed over creation in His life, over death and Hades in His resurrection and which is now seen in the one who is 'far above all principality and power and might and dominion with all things under His feet' (Ephesians 1:21-22). The sceptre which He wields demands the obedience of those He now calls to Himself.

In both the Old and New Testaments, the word translated 'to obey' is closely associated with attentive hearing. In the New Testament, the word literally means 'to hear under.' Listening is involved, and submission to the one whose voice is heard. The Lord Himself, as the obedient Man, daily engaged in attentive and submissive listening to the voice of God (Isaiah 50:4-5), for the law of God was in His heart (Psalm 40:6-8). What He displayed so majestically in His own life, He seeks in those He calls (Matthew 7:24-27), that they too might have open ears, listening attentively to His word and practising its daily observance.

Preaching the kingdom of God

The authority of God and the call to obey Him was at the heart of the message of the Lord Jesus who, at the beginning of His public ministry, 'came to Galilee, preaching the gospel of the kingdom of God' (Mark 1:14). This was the purpose for which He had been sent (Luke 4:43), which He fulfilled in earnest as He 'went through every city and village, preaching and bringing the glad tidings of the kingdom of God' (Luke 8:1; Luke 9:11; Luke 16:16). His message concerned the good news of the prospective fulfilment of God's purposes in Him, that God would gather together a redeemed people for His own possession and make of them a kingdom amongst which His rule would be acknowledged and His will given expression on the earth. This operation of divine rule would not be carried out within the confines of an earthly realm, as it had been in Israel's day (1 Corinthians 15:50); instead, it would be made known through the Holy Spirit to those born anew by redemption in Christ, that by obedience to the Word of God entry into this kingdom might be secured (John 3:3,5).

The message which the apostles received from the Lord also addressed this essential remit (Luke 9:1–2,60; Luke 10:9), not only during the years of His ministry, but also in the witness of the early churches of God. The importance 'of the things pertaining to the kingdom of God' (Acts 1:3) was emphasised in the forty days following His resurrection, when this formed the basis of His teaching to His apostles. So, on the day of Pentecost when the harvest of 3,000 was gathered in, they were ready to act in accordance with the pattern they had received; but more particularly, the teaching of those forty days characterised their gospel preaching throughout the lands in which the churches of God operated as they 'preached the things concerning the kingdom of God and the name of Jesus Christ' (Acts 8:12).

Paul too, who had not been present when the Lord revealed to the apostles 'the mysteries of the kingdom of God' (Luke 8:10), preached this kingdom. In Ephesus, he spent three months 'reasoning and persuading concerning the things of the kingdom of God' (Acts 19:8) not failing to declare 'the whole counsel of God' (Acts 20:25-27) which in coming days the Ephesians would have to defend against wolves creeping in amongst the flock.

Obedience and the call

So the pattern of Biblical evangelism centred on the authority of God and the necessary response it demands. The call of God requires obedience in two ways: first, the hearer must obey the call; and secondly, obedience to the call will bring the hearer into committed, life-long obedience to God. When the God of glory called Abram, 'by faith Abraham obeyed' (Hebrews 11:8). This was Abram's necessary response, but it was not an end in itself, merely the vital first step in a life-long calling to submissive and faithful obedience by which he would meet the desire of God, to 'walk before Me and be blameless' (Genesis 17:1). This pattern in Abraham's experience was repeated in Paul's. Saul of Tarsus was not disobedient to the heavenly vision by which he was called (Acts 26:19), but that initial step committed Paul to permanent allegiance to His Lord whose sovereign authority he now acknowledged, even above the value of his own life, that he might 'finish my race with joy, and the ministry which I received from the Lord Jesus' (Acts 20:24).

The supreme authority of the Lord Jesus demands that those who respond to His call are obedient to Him who called them. Again, the obedience is two-fold. First, the Lord desires a personal obedience borne out of deep gratitude for the saving work of Calvary. The standard is high for it corresponds to an incalculable cost: 'He died for all, that those who live should live no longer for themselves, but for Him who died for them' (2 Corinthians 5:15; 1 Corinthians 6:19-20). This personal obedience must then be displayed in collective obedience which God seeks in a people gathered together and separated according to His will to be moulded by the pattern revealed to them in Scripture. In this, the saints in Rome were commended, that having once been slaves to sin they now 'obeyed from the heart that form of doctrine to which you were delivered' (Romans 6:17).

The image used is that of the foundry, where molten metal is poured into a cast to take the shape of the mould. They had been delivered into the apostles' teaching, known also as the Faith (Jude 1:3) and firmly based in the Lord's own forty-day teaching of Acts 1:3. As a cast, it had shaped them according to God's consistent design to be observed throughout the churches (1 Corinthians 7:17; 1 Corinthians 11:16).

The Gospel call today

Today, the gospel which the apostles preached is in our charge and we will do well to reflect the essence and conviction of their message, declaring at the heart of the gospel the sovereign authority of the Lord and His unanswerable claim on the lives of men. The day will come when the obedience of all the peoples shall be to Him (Genesis 49:10 RV), but until then we proclaim the Lord Jesus who was crucified and has now been made both Lord and Christ (Acts 2:36). In the gospel of God's glory we find the loving invitation and the free gift, but it also comprises the command of a holy God (Acts 17:30) calling men to repentance and obedience. It is not open to us to tell of the loving Saviour, yet omit the conviction call to obedient service.

We must declare the whole counsel of God who has invested His Son with unanswerable authority, issuing the call as He did, and the apostles in His stead, commanding men to respond in attentive obedience to the gospel of the kingdom of God, whereby they may be found under His beneficent rule as servants in the place where His glory dwells.

Bible quotations from the NKJV.

For further study:

1. In what way does the Biblical pattern of evangelism centre on God's authority?
2. If Gospel preaching is to be authentic what must we ensure is included in the message?
3. What does 'taking up our cross daily' for the Lord involve?
4. Should the thrust of our teaching be more 'Jesus as Lord' than 'Jesus as Saviour'?
5. How can lives of personal obedience to the Gospel also display (or share in the display of) collective obedience?

9

Called to Die – Brian Johnston

The policeman leaned forward, placing his elbows on the desk between us. He looked me in the eye, and said in a slow, deliberate manner: "You know what Philippians 1:21 says, don't you?" I had inquired whether it was safe to travel into the interior; to the uplands of the Philippine island where the pot-holed concrete roads give place to rutted tracks which ascend, precariously at times, into the hills. Those hills conceal rebels fighting against the national government, ever on the look-out for opportunistic hostage-taking.

Without so much as pausing to see if I would reply, the duty officer proceeded to answer his own question: "For [you] to live is Christ; to die is gain.'" Then he added, "So what's your problem?" Precautions later suggested by the officer and his colleagues were followed and we did go, and I'm so glad we did. The Church of God in Liguyon is now planted on those green and fertile uplands. What's more, the church company there more than doubled in number in its first six months. Memories of ancestral spirit worship can still be recalled, but theirs is now the joy of worshipping 'in spirit and truth'; some, at least, have really absorbed the biblical revelation (in Hebrews 10:19) that God's gathered people enter the Holy Place in heaven as they worship around the Lord's table each 'Domingo' (or Lord's Day (1 Corinthians 16:1,2; Acts 20:6,7; cf. Revelation 1:10)).

This is a young church that delights in salvation 'by grace ... through faith' (Ephesians 2:8,9), and one that's characterized by sweet singing and thunderous 'Amens'! To sit in their simple bamboo lattice building perched on the mountainside, amid their worship and later to enjoy their child-like response to the Word of God is nothing short of thrilling. The older ones show their commitment by walking for four hours in the sun to remember their Lord; while the youth engage in monthly all-night prayer meetings.

One young servant of Christ who's been so helpful to this fruitful ministry has selflessly expended himself for their progress in the Faith. And he talks about some of their own number who 'work tirelessly' and especially of sisters who give of their time and skills 'voluntarily' for the good of the community. It reminds me of the secret for a fruitful ministry which the Lord Jesus stated in John 12:24-26: 'unless a grain of wheat falls into the earth and dies, it remains alone; but if it dies, it bears much fruit. He who loves his life loses it, and he who hates his life in this world will keep it to life eternal. If anyone serves Me, he must follow Me.'

This is hating one's life in terms of not pursuing the world's applause or approval or even to advance oneself in its estimation. How much better it is to share the Lord's things with child-like hearts than to earn the plaudits of the wise and intelligent or even to be obsessed with 'street cred' in the midst of a 'cool' generation! There's a high cost in discipleship, as the Lord fairly warned His followers: "If anyone wishes to come after Me, he must deny himself and take up Iris cross daily and follow Me" (Luke 9:23).

Surely Dietrich Bonhoeffer was right when he said, 'When Christ calls a man he bids him come and die.' Not necessarily meaning to die physically for the cause of Christ - though it meant that for him, of course, as it has for many others - but to die to our own will, desires and preferences, spurning selfish ambition and all that this world system has to offer in terms of its vain glory. It is to understand that the cross of our Lord Jesus Christ is the means of our being crucified to the world and also it to us (Galatians 6:14). It is to go 'outside the camp' with a world-rejected Saviour (Hebrews 13:13).

Thomas was one of the first disciples whom the Lord called, and he understood something of this. We remember him for his doubts, but let's also remember him for his dedication: 'Thomas, who is called Didymus, said to his fellow disciples, "Let us also go, so that we may die with Him"' (John 11:16). That sets the standard for all disciples of the Lord Jesus Christ from the humid archipelago of the Philippines to the bustling centres of the patronizingly self-styled First World.

Bible quotations from the NASB.

For further study:

1. Contrast Romans 6:23 with Revelation 3:18. How would these support the contention that salvation is free, but discipleship is costly?
2. Matthew 13:46 has often been used to picture the price the Lord paid for us. Does it also speak to the issue of our commitment as disciples?
3. The apostle Paul wrote of 'living sacrifices' in Romans 12:1. Do you think that the presentation of yourself to the Lord envisaged here is once-for-all or ongoing?
4. What do you think going 'outside the camp' (Hebrews 13:13) meant for them – and what does it mean for us?
5. How can you relate to the secret of fruitful ministry in your experience (John 12:24)?

10

Called as Saints – David Woods

Once, when preoccupied with legitimate distractions in Paris' Charles De Gaulle airport, I didn't hear the boarding call for my flight home to Manchester. Right at the last moment I noticed the time, raced to the gate to be greeted by some disgruntled French ground staff. "We've been calling for you. Please board immediately. You're the final passenger." It had been a close call!

God is calling too, but not all hear it. Some hear It, but don't respond as fully as God desires. It's a call to become an integral part of something that is so precious to Him – a call to be found among God's people: His saints who are gathered according to His will. Have you heard it and responded? God's desire for every believer is that they be joined harmoniously with others and together obey the commands of the Lord and follow His teaching as it's been revealed in God's Word. Such believers will be baptised and added to a local church of God, and will enjoy meeting together for fellowship, for prayer, for teaching and for the Remembrance, or the 'Breaking of the Bread'. Such a group of disciples is known as a Church of God (see Acts 2:41-42, 1 Peter 2:4-5, Ephesians 2:19-22; 1 Corinthians 1:2).

Paul greeted the individuals who together formed the local Churches of God in Rome and Corinth as those who were 'called as saints' and 'saints by calling' (Romans 1:7; 1 Corinthians 1:2). Ananias, in his conversation with the Lord during the vision recorded in Acts 9, referred to the early Christians of the Church of God in Jerusalem as 'Your saints' (Acts 9:13). Erroneous teaching has led many to follow a false tradition of recognising individuals of immense spiritual character as 'saints', who attain such a status only when their lives are reviewed by others after death. How far from the truth this is! God's Word reveals to us that those at Rome and Corinth were 'saints by calling.'

Looking at the original New Testament language brings us a proper sense of what the word 'saints' really means. The Greek foundation (hagios) is a word that denotes something 'sacred' or 'holy', and is elsewhere simply translated as 'holy'. It's logical, then, to read 'saints' as 'holy ones.' When we place this alongside the wonderful scriptures of Ephesians 1 - 'He chose us in Him before the foundation of the world, that we would be holy and blameless before Him' (Ephesians 1:4) - we gain an altogether superior view of what 'saints by calling' conveys. It's not a designation based on an assessment made by man, but an eternal calling of God.

Of course, holiness is something that God desires from every believer. Our personal holiness facilitates a closeness of ongoing relationship with a holy God. As individuals, we are to be set apart to Him, and separate from the defilement of a corrupting world. When Paul wrote to the saints in Corinth he encouraged them with the words - let us cleanse ourselves from all defilement of flesh and spirit, perfecting holiness in the fear of God (2 Corinthians 7:1). Paul knew, all too well, the great struggle we have in maintaining personal holiness before our holy God. Defilement affects our 'flesh' and our 'spirit' and can lead to ruin. How right Paul was not to mention the 'soul' in that verse - our souls have been forever cleansed and made holy by the atoning work of Christ - it's in our bodies and minds before God that we're required to give effect to our salvation with fear and trembling (Philippians 2:12).

We know those things that defile our flesh and spirit, but we're often guilty of continuing in them. How can we guard ourselves against such defilement? Some suggestions might be:

1. attempting to consciously live each moment appreciating the reality of the presence of God. If we know that the Holy Spirit indwells us and we seek to allow him to have His influence in all that we do, then our lives lived under such moment-by-moment direction will be holy lives.

2. laying hold of the wonderful promise of 1 John 1:9 'If we confess our sins, He is faithful and righteous to forgive us our sins and to cleanse us from all unrighteousness.' True and sincere confession and repentance before God removes the stains of sin. To confess to Him we must be speaking with Him - prayer is vital if we are to be holy people.

3. spending time in God's Word, reading His repeated calls for His people to be holy. This will show us the true standards by which we should live our lives-God clearly tells us what's expected! We're encouraged to 'consider Jesus' and to run 'fixing our eyes on Jesus' (Hebrews 3:1; Hebrews 12:2). He's the benchmark.

4. pre-worship self-assessment. The people of God have the great privilege of worshipping God in the Holy Place. From Psalm 24 we learn that only those with 'clean hands' and 'pure hearts' (cf. 'flesh and spirit') can ascend the hill of the Lord and stand in His holy place. The weekly practice of reviewing the state of our lives in the knowledge that we will enter God's holy presence will have a profound impact on our lives.

'For this is the will of God, your sanctification ... that each of you know how to possess his own vessel in sanctification and honor ... God has not called us for the purpose of impurity, but in sanctification' (1 Thessalonians 4:3-7). Vine tells us that 'sanctification is used of separation to God ... the separation of the believer from evil things and ways.'[6] This is what we've been called to; this is the will of God!

Holiness is something God desires of every believer, but His purposes don't stop there. He wants believers to enjoy what it means to be 'called as saints' -and so to live out lives of

---

[6] W.E. Vine, Vine's Complete Expository Dictionary of Old & New Testament Words

holiness alongside others. Look back at 1 Corinthians 1:2 and we'll notice that Paul reminds the saints that they are 'those who have been sanctified in Christ Jesus, saints by calling.' It takes us back to the Old Testament time when God brought Israel out of Egyptian slavery. They were called out that they might be His holy people, a holy nation, a people who together would worship Him. He separated them from their past lives, gave them His commandments for holy living and constituted them as His holy nation when they accepted His covenant and were 'separated' to Him (Deuteronomy 7:6; Leviticus 19:2; Exodus 19:5). This was all a shadow of what God does today with those released from the slavery of sin. He gives freedom so that we might, by subsequently obeying His laws and His commands, form His holy people. Read 1 Peter 2:4-10 again!

When Paul was writing his letters to the Church of God in Corinth he was dealing with some serious sins and unholy practices that were being accepted by the Church. At the outset, Paul reminded them that they were 'holy ones by calling.' It was only right that any blatant and tolerated sin was exposed and dealt with appropriately through discipline and ultimately excommunication of those caught up in the sin. The holiness of God's people had to be taken seriously. They had to learn what it meant to be sanctified in Christ Jesus. The same applies today. Those who are 'called as saints' have a personal, and collective responsibility, to demonstrate God's standard of holiness in a world that is so full of sin.

A good place to finish is Ephesians 1:18 - "I pray that the eyes of your heart may be enlightened, so that you will know what is the hope of His calling, what are the riches of the glory of His inheritance in the saints. God calls us to be 'saints.'" Let's strive to be the holy ones He has called us to be.

Bible quotations from the NASB.

For further study:

1. How, in practice, do the four suggestions for holy living help us to live up to our responsibility - both personal and collective - to demonstrate our status as saints by God's calling?
2. How would you distinguish between your inheritance in Christ and God's inheritance in His people?
3. Are you surprised by the emphasis or priority placed on holiness in 1 Thessalonians 4:3 when Paul was proceeding to instruct on a Christian's lifestyle?
4. The believers in the Church of God at Corinth were addressed as being 'holy ones' ('saints'), but almost immediately the apostle Paul begins to take issue with their unholy behaviours. How does this help us to see that we are to become in daily living what we already are 'in Christ'?
5. How has this chapter helped you to distinguish holiness that is a) in Christ, b) in daily living, and c) in and among God's people?

11

Called to Share a Heavenly Calling – Keith Dorricott

Jim Hayhurst, in his book 'The Right Mountain'[7] describes what it's like to be on an expedition to climb Mount Everest, the highest mountain on earth. Reaching the summit is paramount and all efforts are devoted to achieving that. Along the way there can be many difficulties and setbacks, but what keeps the team going is the prospect of 'getting to the top.' He says that, when the going gets tough, you don't lower your sights, you just increase your support. At one point in their climb, this involved the team tying themselves to the side of a vertical cliff three thousand feet high, in order to have a place to sleep to be able to make it to the summit. It was either that or go back. He said that they certainly made sure those ties were very secure! Eventually the team made it to the top.

During this course we have been exploring what is involved in

---

[7] Jim Hayhurst Sr., The Right Mountain: Lessons From Everest On the Real Meaning of Success, John Wiley & Sons, 1992

pursuing our calling from God as disciples of the Lord Jesus Christ. There are many causes to which we can devote our lives; many inspiring challenges; many worthy endeavours. Younger people in particular are often urged to find out what their passion is and then pursue it to the full, to make the most of life. But the calling that we have been given far exceeds the best of those, whether we realise it or not. The Lord of heaven is calling us to go to the very top, to have the highest experience possible for human beings, and to give ourselves entirely to it. What a tragedy if we miss it!

The Lord Jesus is now engaged in the gathering together of what He knows His Father longs to have - true worshippers who will worship Him in spirit and truth (John 4:24), not here on earth as used to be the case, but now in heaven itself, where He is. Imagine us going into heaven to worship God there! This in fact is what we are called to do – it is a 'heavenly calling' (Hebrews 3:1). This purpose is occupying Christ in the building up of a house for God, bringing together a people for that purpose, to be worshippers who together offer up to His God and Father spiritual sacrifices (1 Peter 2:5). Because we are still living on earth, we gather for our worship times in locations here, but what we are actually engaging in spiritually is very much in heaven itself, where God is. As God's Son, Christ is building this house, over which He has been given total authority; and as the man Jesus He serves as its high priest (Hebrews 5:1-5). He is the one who acts on behalf of the worshipping people, and represents them before His God and Father in the very throne room of heaven.

In all this he is totally faithful (Hebrews 2:17), just as He was in His life on earth, totally reliable in everything that pertains to God, leaving nothing undone. The question is: how faithful are the worshippers that He wants to bring? How is each of us as a believer in Jesus Christ responding to this heavenly call? Because we are not guaranteed this privilege - it requires our faithfulness, too (Hebrews 3:6). What if we lose sight of the top? Or what if we've never seen it and don't realize that it is there for us to reach? What if our awareness of our calling is very limited? What in fact must we do in order to be part of this privileged company, to be one of the active partakers of our heavenly calling?

The first thing we must do is come to Christ to be built into this spiritual house. We are already believers in Christ, but we must also put ourselves under the one who has the full authority as Son over God's house (Hebrews 3:6). We do this when, as genuine disciples, we are baptized into the name of the Father and the Son and the Holy Spirit (giving Christ His rightful place), and then are added to a church of God to become part of those who together serve Him in His house (Matthew 28:19; Acts 2:41; 1 Timothy 3:15).

Then we must continually hold fast to the confession of our hope (Hebrews 4:14; Hebrews 10:23). This is the confession of Christ, as the one who makes this worship possible. If we lose that confession of our hope, we can lose the privilege of being part of the house of God (Hebrews 3:6). We will have missed being part of the team that goes to the top. The epistle to the Hebrews refers to five ways it is possible to lose it - we can drift away due to neglect, we can fall away due to unbelief, we can throw it away by undervaluing it, we can turn away from it due to other pressures, or we can be carried away from it by the influence of others (Hebrews 2:1; Hebrews 3:12; Hebrews 10:35; Hebrews 12:25; Hebrews 13:9). These are all obstacles to our heavenly calling.

And then, as we gather together for our times of worship, when in the churches of God we remember the Lord Jesus in the bread and wine, we 'draw near to God in heaven in full assurance of faith' (Hebrews 10:22). As we do this, do we truly realise where we are spiritually, and what we are doing? This is far removed from our surroundings here on earth. And it isn't just in our imagination, it is realizing the reality of it - we are at the pinnacle! What reverence and what exhilaration that should inspire in us - every single time! Even though we don't understand it fully, by faith we appreciate it. God has said it and so we believe it to be true. We draw near to God, not out of ritual or duty, but out of sincere and full hearts. Without the assurance that faith provides, our worship meetings will be deadly dull and a waste of time. If we treat it casually, or our minds are somewhere else, or we don't realize what is truly going on, we'll be muddling along farther down the mountain, not at all experiencing the pinnacle.

Mountain climbing is not easy. It takes a lot of preparation, and a lot of persistence. When the team is on the climb and the going gets very hard, some of them may be tempted to give up. But ask Jim Hayhurst, or anyone who has made it to the top, whether it was all worth it and they are in no doubt. Our calling as disciples of Jesus Christ can similarly involve sacrifices and difficulty. Some of the modules have examined that side of it - the humility required in serving, the need to be prepared to suffer, if necessary, and the self-denial. There are costs to true discipleship. Compromise isn't an option. We may object to the confinement of being in something that the world regards very lightly, when seemingly more attractive options are being offered. These may tempt us to settle for something less than the full privileges of our calling. But, as Jim Hayhurst reminds us, we must not lose sight of the top. We must hold on to our confession of hope, by expressing it to God - by actually confessing it (just as Jesus did faithfully before Pilate, despite all the pressures to save his own skin (1 Timothy 6:13)).

Finally, what do we do when we are there? We offer our sacrifices - 'Through Him then, let us continually offer up a sacrifice of praise to God, that is, the fruit of lips that give thanks to His name' (Hebrews 13:15). Worship is not just having an emotionally stimulating time, perhaps with musical performances. Worship is expressing to God our appreciation of Him and His Son, to the fullest extent that we are able, so that God receives from His redeemed creatures what he cannot give Himself- true worship. Worship is all about giving. All the focus is on Him and His Son. As we stand at the summit, and survey the majesty around us, it humbles us, and thrills us. We have seen the majesty of our God! We have given to Him what He longs for, but we feel all the benefit. That is what we are being offered, fellow-partakers, a heavenly calling!

Bible quotations from the NASB.

For further study:

1. How can we be sure of being part of 'the team' that goes to the top?
2. How is the faithfulness of Jesus still being expressed today?
3. Many references from Hebrews have been used in this section. This Bible letter draws extensively from the Old Testament illustration of God's tabernacle 'house' and definite pattern for worship. How does all this background add to the sense of 'build-up' for the experience described in this final chapter?
4. Describe in your own words how we can survey the majesty of God standing at the summit as we worship in spirit and in truth.

12

Called to Possess God's Hope – Leonard Ross

Do you have any financial investments? If not, you'll have been spared a lot of the anxiety and disappointment that those who do, experience from time to time. But what about God - does He have investments? He who owns 'the cattle on a thousand hills ... the world is Mine and all its fullness' has no need to invest in material things (Psalm 50:10,12). But He does invest in people, and if you are His child, having responded to His call through the gospel, He has invested in you. 'He who did not spare His own Son, but delivered Him up for us all, how shall He not with Him also freely give us all things?' (Romans 8:32) - what an investment!

But it's a poor investment that gives no return, and surely God expects one on His investment, and He will, of course, get this! There will come a day when Father and Son will see 'the labor of [the Son's] soul, and be satisfied' (Isaiah 53:11), when the 'eternal purpose which He accomplished in Christ Jesus our Lord' is fully realised (Ephesians 3:11). But what about 'today'?

Previous modules have described the many spiritual blessings made available to those who are 'in Christ' not least of which is our 'hope' and our 'inheritance'. Peter tells us about these - God in His mercy has 'begotten us again to a living hope through the resurrection of Jesus Christ from the dead, to an inheritance incorruptible and undefiled and that does not fade away, reserved in heaven for you' (1 Peter 1:3-4); these are absolute certainties. But God also has a 'hope' and an 'inheritance', and that's what this final module is about. Paul's prayer for the saints in the church in Ephesus was 'that you may know what is the hope of His calling, what are the riches of the glory of His inheritance in the saints, and what is the exceeding greatness of His power toward us who believe' (Ephesians 1:18-19).

Robert Louis Stevenson wrote, 'To travel hopefully is a better thing than to arrive', and you can perhaps understand what he meant. However, that's not true of Christians. To 'arrive' for them will be very far better than the journey they have taken through life's experiences! But what Stevenson wrote begs the question of those of us who are Christians: just how are we 'travelling' in our journey as disciples of the Lord Jesus? God has an expectation that our redeemed lives will respond fully to His call. The first module referred to the 'purpose of the call and its place in the scheme of things ... given in Romans 8:28-29.' How is it that all things work together for good to those who love God? Sometimes life's experiences don't seem to match such a statement, do they? It's because 'whom He foreknew, He also predestined ... these He also called ... justified ... glorified.' What was His eternal purpose? That those whom He called would be 'conformed to the image of His Son, that He might be the firstborn among many brethren' (Romans 8:29,30).

Let's just try to understand this uplifting truth, that for the Son to be 'firstborn' - that title of excellence - He needs us: all of us who since Calvary are 'in Christ' have responded to the call to salvation. This, in turn, involves something which is a great mystery to us: the sovereignty of God and human responsibility. There are some things that with our finite understanding we just have to accept by faith, and worship the God and the Father of the Lord Jesus Christ! It's true that at salvation we are, in God's view, already 'conformed', for 'whoever has been born of God does not sin' (1 John 3:9), but the reality is that daily we have a battle with our 'flesh' and the real challenge is daily to show that we are indeed trying with best endeavour to conform ourselves by living in a Christ-like way. And so there are...

Things that accompany salvation

God's hope, or expectation in His calling through the gospel is that we will 'work out [our] own salvation with fear and trembling' (Philippians 2:12); this does not give us licence to do this as we please. The Lord has provided a blueprint for disciple service. We must be clear that no service enhances in any sense the security of our eternal salvation, but Peter writes about the need to be 'diligent to make [our] call and election sure ... for so an entrance will be supplied to you abundantly into the everlasting kingdom of our Lord and Savior Jesus Christ' (2 Peter 1:10-11), diligent to live in such a way as to 'adorn the doctrine of God our Savior in all things' (Titus 2:10).

When the Lord during the forty days met with the apostles

He was 'speaking of the things pertaining to the kingdom of God' (Acts 1:3), this was not the 'everlasting kingdom' to which Peter referred, but a kingdom composed of obedient disciples, united in corporate service according to the pattern of Acts 2:41-42, and as valid and fundamental in 2009 as it was back then. Even further back in time, we can read in Deuteronomy 32:9 that 'the Lord's portion is His people; Jacob is the place of His inheritance' and, dependent upon their obedience to God's covenant then, Israel would be identified as a 'kingdom of priests and a holy nation' (Exodus 19:5-6). The New Testament spiritual counterpart is what the Lord taught His apostles, and which then became known as 'the apostles' teaching', the basis for collective service of disciples then, and now.

God has an expectation in His calling that redeemed lives will respond to Him and give their lives in service, and in corporate testimony be found as His inheritance today. Yes, we do have an inheritance, guaranteed, but so does God, and Paul's longing was that the disciples in Ephesus would be given that 'spirit of wisdom and revelation ... [their] understanding being enlightened' to know this, and appreciate this as they served the Lord there (Ephesians 1:17,18).

Along with the great panoramic view of the truths of the Body of Christ throughout the Scriptures and the eternal purpose which God purposed in His Son, let us be aware that He also has a present purpose - as in Old Testament times in a gathered-together and identifiable people today. In an increasingly liberal Christian society, fundamental doctrine is not really the in thing', and of course we all face the challenge of what, some-times, seems 'compromise', but here is the encouragement to try, by His grace and with His power to be…

Fit for purpose

Fit for purpose – 'the fulfilment of a specification' is one definition. Those 'whom He called' are intended here and now to meet the 'specification' of 'conformed to the image of His Son' (Romans 8:29,30), and the wonderful call through the gospel envisages a life of service from those who respond, requiring of us, like Paul, to 'testify to the gospel of the grace of God …preaching the kingdom of God … [declaring] the whole counsel of God' (Acts 20:24-27) Worthy of God's 'investment' in us? Giving Him a return? Fit for His purpose in us?

Bible quotations from the NKJV.

For further study:

1. What return does God expect us to make?
2. How would you distinguish between your inheritance in Christ and God's inheritance in His people?
3. How would you distinguish between your hope in Christ and God's hope in His people?
4. What would you say is God's present purpose in having a people on earth?

13

Epilogue

The Lord defined true discipleship when He said, "If anyone wishes to come after Me, he must deny himself, and take up his cross daily and follow Me" (Luke 9:23 NASB). Christ's challenge is threefold, requiring a conscious decision on our part, self-denial and total commitment. The stakes are so high and yet the Lord leaves it to us: "if anyone wishes ..." What powerful imagery the Lord uses, because the man who picked up a cross was no longer living for this world. He no longer had any remaining interest in this world. The committed Christian selflessly loses his life in this world for Christ's sake.

The Lord expects without commanding that we 'come after' Him, to walk in the 'narrow' way with Him, in true freedom enjoying life in all its fullness. Surely with sadness, in view of His supreme sacrifice, the Lord said that only few (believers) are willing so to do. Our various contributing authors have fairly and squarely placed before us these radical demands of genuine discipleship. We should also, however, emphasize the balancing perspective which is that the loss from all this dying to self and to the world is nothing compared with the gain of being altogether taken up with Christ in the power of a Spirit-filled life in which we know God by experience and enjoy the Lord personally!

Real commitment is the measure of real faith. The faith of the early disciples was nothing short of revolutionizing; transforming and moulding their entire lives for the Master. Today pseudo-faith is often reflected in pseudo- commitment. To recap, the challenge throughout this book has been: are we living in the midst of secular society in a manner consistent with the fact that the truth of God possesses our hearts? Do our lives, not merely our words, express the fact that Jesus is real?

We hope your journey through this course will be used by God to re-kindle a desire for a more authentic, biblical discipleship to be expressed in our lives. With the various presented aspects of discipleship now in review, it should be clear that God's design for our discipleship is not only intensely practical (as well as potentially fulfilling!) at a personal level, but as we view it biblically there is a vital dimension of discipleship that can only be realized when we interact with other disciples in a way that sees the New Testament record of the earliest disciples as not merely descriptive but as also being prescriptive for us.

Looking back over some of the later modules especially reinforces the biblical case for such a thing as a pattern for Christian discipleship. If you would like to research that aspect further, we recommend you to take a look at the recommended resources at the end of this book. You can also visit www.churchesofgod.info as you pursue your studies – may God richly bless you!

About Hayes Press

Hayes Press (www.hayespress.org) is a registered charity in the United Kingdom, whose primary mission is to disseminate the Word of God, mainly through literature. It is one of the largest distributors of gospel tracts and leaflets in the United Kingdom, with over 100 titles and many thousands dispatched annually. In addition to paperbacks and eBooks, Hayes Press also publishes Golden Bells, a popular daily Bible reading calendar.

If you would like to contact Hayes Press, there are a number of ways you can do so:

By mail: c/o The Barn, Flaxlands, Royal Wootton Bassett, Wiltshire, UK SN4 8DY

By phone: 01793 850598

By eMail: info@hayespress.org

via Facebook: www.facebook.com/hayespress.org

Also by Hayes Press

Healthy Churches: God's Bible Blueprint for Growth

Many churches in the Western world seem to be declining in numbers and spiritual vitality. Brian explores some of the root causes and also how this trend could be reversed. The good news, as Brian reminds us, is that God gives us the growth blueprint in His Word through a number of key Bible words, such as sowing, reaping, planting, watering, cultivating, building and edifying. Find out the importance of each step in the process and get inspired to go for growth with, in and through, God!

Back to Basics: A Study of Core Bible Teaching and Practice

This book uses a combination of theological and practical content and study questions to explore 8 key topics that are essential to the Christian faith: Knowing God, Salvation, Believer's Baptism, The Breaking of Bread, Understanding The Bible, The Return of Jesus Christ, Spiritual Gifts and Church Life. With study questions for each of the 8 topics as an appendix, this book is ideal for personal or group Bible study.

Different Discipleship: Jesus' Sermon On The Mount

A practical, challenging study (complete with questions and prayer prompts) of the "Sermon on the Mount" for followers and would-be followers of Jesus. What makes Jesus and his followers "different"? Find out why this revolutionary, life-changing sermon is why Jesus Christ is regarded as one of the world's most important teachers, even by those who don't follow him as their Lord and Saviour.